Stürtz REGIO

EAST FRISIA
AND THE
ISLANDS

Text by
Hartmut Schwerdtfeger

Photos by
Günter Franz

OSTFRIESLAND

Ostfriesche

Borkum

Juist

Norderney

Baltrum

Norderney

Neßmersiel

Dornumer

Borkum

Norddeich

Norden

9

Westermarsch

70

Marienhafe

Greetsiel

4

10

Pilsum

Moordorf

Groothusen

3

Upleward

Pewsum

8

Ihlow

46

Rysum

6

2 Emden

Ditzum

Jemgum

NL

Bunde

1 Buddelschiff-Museum

2 Feuerschiff „Deutsche Bucht"
(v.a. gutes Fisch-Restaurant)

3 Freilichtmuseum Manningaburg

4 Schönster Sielhafen

5 Inselmuseum „Alter Leuchtturm"

6 Kunsthalle

7 Moor- und Fehnmuseum Elisabethfehn

8 Ostfriesisches Landesmuseum

9 Ostfriesisches Teemuseum

10 Marienhafe, Störtebekerturm

Weener

70

31

Papen

Spiekerook

5

Wangerooge

I n s e l n

ngeoog

ngeoog

Neuharlingersiel

Harlesiel

Minsen

Bensersiel

1

Carolinensiel

Esens

Wittmund

210

Jever

Middels

Schortens

urich

Friedeburg

Wiesmoor

Zetel

Bockhorn

Wilhelms-
haven

Sande

29

28

Westerstede

Apen

Barßel

72

7

Bad
Zwischenahn

Oldenburg

Edewecht

| 0 | 5 | 10 | 15 | 20 km |

Stürtz REGIO

EAST FRISIA
AND THE
ISLANDS

Text by
Hartmut Schwerdtfeger

Photos by
Günter Franz

Top front cover:
Leer harbour
Bottom front cover:
fisherman,
the dunes,
farmhouse gable

Back cover
and p. 4/5:
Pilsum lighthouse

P. 8/9:
flourishing trade
was once a sure sign
of wealth.
Leer harbour with
its splendid town
hall is a witness to
past affluence.

The Authors

Hartmut Schwerdtfeger, a journalist and the author of much regional literature on Northern Germany, lives near Bremen.

Günter Franz is a freelance photographer in Bremen.

Credits

Photos:
Archiv für Kunst und Geschichte, Berlin:
p. 30 (top right), 31 (top), 36 (bottom).

Die Deutsche Bibliothek–CIP catalogue record
East Frisia / Günter Franz (photographer),
Hartmut Schwerdtfeger (author). –
Würzburg: Stürtz 1998.
ISBN 3-8003-1022-8 / paperback

Design: Förster Illustration & Grafik, Rimpar
Cartography: Steffen Oberländer, Munich
Repro: Hofmüller, Linz
Translation: Ruth Chitty, Saulheim
Printed and edited by the Universitätsdruckerei
H. Stürtz AG, Würzburg

ISBN 3-8003-1022-8 / paperback

All of Günter Franz's photos were taken with Leica cameras.

CONTENTS

THE FACES OF EAST FRISIA

Once upon a time the ocean was lapping against the shore of the North Sea coast when it came face to face with an East Frisian. It drew back in horror, and since then has cautiously rolled back twice a day to see if the coast is clear. This is how high and low tide came about ...

This is just one of the many jokes about East Frisians

popular among Germans several years back, and still not entirely out of fashion. Some of them are quite funny, others less so – and some not at all. Yet they all have one thing in common; they fail to affect the East Frisians in two ways. They neither characterise the East Frisian mentality, nor are the subjects of the jokes in the least bothered by them. The East Frisians faced this wave of humour with composure, as they do the waves of the North Sea. And not without reason. The people on the coast are ruled by the elements – far more so than their landlubber cousins.

Over the centuries the sea and the wind have carved their signatures on the faces and souls of the East Frisians.

The sea has given, and the sea has taken away. It has claimed its victims, both people and land. Man is almost powerless

against the forces of Nature, and this has heavily moulded the East Frisian character.

In an attempt to tame the elements, the protection of the coastline was made a national concern in the 1960s and suitable funding provided, resulting in dykes becoming higher and safer. This was a positive move; other changes to the region have been less beneficial. Fishing, agriculture and the shipping and shipbuilding industry have lost their once strong grip on the economy. There are fewer and fewer jobs for people in these sectors. To date, insufficient alternatives are available. The sparsely-populated north-west of Germany is considered to be lacking in infrastructure.

East Frisia's deficient economic and cultural exchange with other regions does have a more positive side – a certain stability.

Wind was the main source of energy on the wide plains of East Frisia for a long time. The windmill in Riepe is a relic of former times.

Seagulls – ever-present coastline companions. The way they use the wind in flight is extremely skilful and almost playful.

The people here and their land have changed at a much slower rate than the densely-populated industrial centres and major cities elsewhere in Germany. This is undoubtedly the reason for East Frisia's authentic charm. The character of the area and its people is basically much as it always was. It is this which draws holidaymakers seeking peace and quiet. Tourism, the "invisible economy", has become one of the major pillars of the East Frisian economy. For centuries the islands have had their very own enthusiastic clientele, many of whom come back year after year.

More and more people have also discovered the unique appeal of the wide, green plateaux with their sleepy villages and farms, their many tiny brooks and streams, fishing villages and ancient towns.

East Frisia has a lot more to offer

than just relaxation and tranquillity. If it's variety you're looking for, you'll find it here. If you really want to get to know the country and its people, you'll find plenty of warm, friendly souls to help you, especially if you undertake your East Frisian explorations off the beaten tourist track or out of season. You'll come to love and appreciate this part of the country – and you'll come back here. But keep your eyes open and be prepared to search a little for the true, endearing character of the area. East Frisia is not a lexicon of superlatives; it thrives on a peacefulness and serenity which are truly captivating. The wind and the sea have not been the only things to hit the East Frisians hard in the past; history has also ravaged the area.

At its most expansive, the region stretched to the Ijsselmeer in the west and the Lower Weser River in the east. Today, East Frisia covers a much smaller surface area stretching from the Dutch border to the city gates of Oldenburg. Yet this reduction in size has failed to diminish the pride of the East Frisians. In fact, they consider territories lost over the years "renegade areas". The East Frisians are pretty touchy in this respect. If a stranger makes the mistake of counting the Jeverland or Oldenburg as part of East Frisia when talking to one of the older locals, then he or she shouldn't be surprised if their interlocutor suddenly goes quiet ...

There is one generous exception to the above question of modern territorial borders:

Wangerooge, the most eastern of the East Frisian islands. East Frisia's boundaries are clearly determined by those of the Aurich district. Wangerooge doesn't lie within these boundaries; it belongs to the Oldenburg district. Yet it is an obvious component in the chain of East Frisian islands – according to the East Frisians. Wangerooge is thus an East Frisian island which isn't – at least not for administrative purposes.

Crooked church towers, like this one in Suurhusen near Emden, are not an uncommon sight in East Frisia. The soft, marshy soil has often given way to the pressure of bricks and mortar.

Aurich is the centre of East Frisia. Not because it is the seat of regional administration, but because "it always was". This is historically not quite accurate, but nevertheless how the people here see things. To the south-west of the town is

Upstalsboom, a regional relic from long ago.

Upstalsboom was a meeting place where Frisians practised an early form of democracy. Roman historian Tacitus wrote of Upstalsboom: "At gatherings everyone takes his place with his weapons as he desires. If a proposal meets with disapproval, it is cast out amongst much grumbling; if it meets with favour, spears are shaken..." Tacitus also wrote at length of the unassailable desire for free-

dom the Teutons, and thus also the Frisians, displayed. Roman commander Varus was unable to conquer Lower Germany. In an attempt to do so, his proud legions were annihilated in the battles fought in the Teutoburg Forest. A stone pyramid at Upstalsboom is East Frisia's 19th-century monument to this drive for freedom and independence.

Aurich, first a tribal seat, then a royal residency and now the region's centre of administration, lies at the heart of East Frisia. The wide, flat, East Frisian plains accommodate few towns.

Wittmund, Esens and Norden are to the north. Emden to the south-west is the largest town in the area. Leer, Weener and Papenburg line the Ems River to the south. Few and far between, they are all worth a visit and compact in their layout. All boast lively, interesting architectural forms in their medieval town centres. History is paired with the modern traits of town life and mirrored in the town buildings, seldom spectacular but notable despite their modest scale. The Dutch influence is omnipresent.

The proximity of The Netherlands is very noticeable in East Frisia. Many canals have Dutch-style wooden draw-bridges, like here in Papenburg in the Emsland.

The East Frisian countryside is literally as flat as a pancake. Cynics joke that "you can see who's coming to pay a Sunday visit on Wednesday". This, of course, isn't quite true, for the view out across the plateau is broken up by gentle elevations, wide valleys, moors and lakes, winding dykes and numerous clumps of trees. Lonely farms, built on artificial mounds to protect them from floods, block the view with their typical low, wide roofs. The deepest "valleys" are a mere 7.5 feet below sea level.

The highest elevations don't even reach 100 feet.

Small lakes are called *Meere,* such as the Frauenmeer or Große Meer, to avoid confusion with the North Sea (German *Nordsee*).

All clichés pertaining to the East Frisian countryside are fulfilled by the area known as Krumm-hörn – for East Frisian connoisseurs and fanatics, this is the epitome of East Frisia. The Stör-tebeker-Strasse from Emden to Greetsiel crosses this scenic peninsula. It is best explored by

bicycle or on foot away from the main roads.

The coast between the Ems and Jade estuaries is lined with one pretty little fishing village after another. The villages sprang up around harbour sluices built to keep the North Sea from flowing into natural inland water channels and causing flooding. Greetsiel, set in a sea bay (Ley-bucht) near the mouth of the Ems, acts as a magnet for visitors. Its twin windmills, visible from far and wide, are a local landmark. The fishing villages still operate, with cutters regularly setting out to sea to catch the area's tastiest inhabitants: plaice, expensive sole and prawns and shrimps. The harbours also run ferry services to the islands off shore: Wangerooge, Spiekeroog, Langeoog, Baltrum, Norderney, Juist and Borkum, sand dunes formed by the elements and sculpted into East Frisian islands.

Even in the winter East Frisia is not completely devoid of tourists. This ship is leaving Harlesiel, on course for Wangerooge.

Wangerooge, Spiekeroog, Langeoog, Baltrum, Norderney, Juist and Borkum

Thousands of holiday-makers each year enjoy themselves on long, sandy beaches on the north side of the islands. Behind them slope the steep sand dunes with their often sparse vegetation, protecting the island dwellers and their houses from the wind

Sun, sea and sand are what make the North Sea attractive to young and old.

wards. The islands are separated from the coast by mud flats, or the Wattenmeer. At low tide the sea bed is almost completely exposed, a feast for millions of sea birds. Looking at the grey silt, one can hardly believe that it is actually home to a huge variety of aquatic species. Tours of the mud flats with experts offer a lively insight into this animal world. Mud flats like these are only found on the

and the sea in the less friendly months of the year between October and March. Yet there is no ultimate form of protection against nature. Neither the sand dunes nor the artificial bulwarks erected on the western flanks of the islands can withstand the elements for ever. Storms and flooding barrage the islands; bits of land are often sucked back into the sea. The shape of the islands is undergoing a continuous metamorphosis, with the islands themselves shifting slightly east-

North Sea coast. They are biologically unique and have thus been protected as a nature reserve called the Naturpark Niedersächsisches Wattenmeer. The wind and the sea have not only unmistakably shaped the countryside and inhabitants of East Frisia, they will also determine the nature of a holiday in Northern Germany. Of course there are areas in Germany which are windier and wetter. Yet you can't expect to spend two or three weeks here com-

pletely free of wind and rain. They are simply part of life up here, just as much as the wide sky, the lush green, the sea and its people. Variety is the spice of life. Light plays on the land, ever changing, and brings with it a whole spectrum of different moods and colours. East Frisia is different in cloud and in sunlight, in the evening and in the morning, in the summer and in the winter, an interesting interplay of light and weather.

And as far as the East Frisians are concerned, there is no such thing as bad weather – just unsuitable clothing.

If the weather should be a little turbulent, then there's nothing better than a pot of tea in an East Frisian café – not just any old brew but East Frisian tea from one of the local tea companies. These are the only brands which satisfy local palates.

Ostfriesenmischung should be strong with plenty of taste and aroma. According to tradition it is served in the pot and kept warm on a teapot stand heated with a night-light candle. You drink it with brown sugar crystals the East Frisians call *Kluntjes* and a few drops of cream. With the wind howling outside, there's nothing better. ▧

Beach huts were the first seaside changing rooms. This well-preserved example on Wangerooge reminds us of days gone by.

The constant sea breeze is ideal for flying kites.

Aurich is the political centre of East Frisia. The charming Pingelhus, built around 1800 and once a shipping agency on the old harbour, was used to dispatch passengers on their journey until around 1930. The »pingeln« or ringing of the bell announced the next departure of horse-drawn ships to Emden (top left).

Main photo: the administrative heart of rural East Frisian life, representing the gentry, townsfolk and farming communities. Once a political power which could levy taxes and make laws, it is now a public body with 49 full members, seven county officers and one president. Art on the market place (centre left) and the pleasant pedestrian precinct (bottom left).

The Schloss, a product of Historicism built between 1851 and 1855 (top right), is today used by the local council.

18

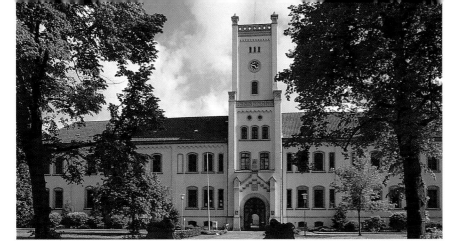

Previous double spread: endless stretches of lowland are a typical sight in East Frisia. An almost secretive serenity hangs over the autumnal landscape.

The moors are no longer the economic cornerstone of the north. Yet the memory of peat farming lives on in the Moorland Museum. Peat villages were poor; peat farming (bottom left) barely earned enough to feed the family. This is also illustrated by the moorland cottages in the "Museum of Poverty" in the peat village near Aurich (top centre). The living room may have been small and humble, but it was always spick-and-span (main photo).

Wattle and bricks are common building materials in Lower Saxon farmhouses.

BOSSELN AND KLOOTSCHEETEN

The uninhibited visitor to East Frisia will probably come across several rather unusual kinds of sport here completely unknown on non-East Frisian terrain. This certainly goes for East Frisia's traditional sporting activities, although the locals also play other, more familiar sports; the absence of tennis and golf from the region is unthinkable since Boris Becker and Bernhard Langer, as is the absence of football. Globalisation has failed to halt at the borders to East Frisia. In theory, golf could be compared to one very popular local sport known as *Boßeln*.

Boßeln is a rather unusual sport peculiar to East Frisia.

As with golf, here you have to concentrate on moving a ball over a certain distance with the least possible goes. Yet the sports differ in practice; with *Boßeln*, the ball is made of wood and between 3 $^1/_2$ and 4 inches in diameter, and it is thrown and not hit with a club. And the "pitch" is also rather different. No beautifully landscaped golf course here – the street suffices. *Boßeln* is a team sport and has many fans throughout East Frisia. Many of them play in *Boßeln* clubs who ambitiously compete against each other to find out who are the *Boßeln* masters of the year.

Klootscheeten is not nearly as popular as *Boßeln* in East Frisia. This is also true of a third sport exclusive to the coast, namely *Schlickrutschen* or "mud-flat sledging".

This rather more modern type of sport originally had little in common with leisure activities and sporting competitions. In former times the sport's wooden contraption, similar to an Eskimo sledge pulled by dogs, was used to transport people and things across the boggy mud-flats.

Modern-day Schlick-rutschen is much kinder to dogs.

The craft is propelled solely by the leg power of its (human) driver. He stands at the back of the sledge and moves his contraption like a child riding its scooter, with one leg providing the momentum and one firmly on the sledge. This demands great strength, for the mud flats are not nearly as smooth and slippery as snow or ice.

Guests in East Frisia who are lucky enough to watch mud-flat sledgers in action are especially delighted when the sledge drivers are so covered in dark brown sludge that one can hardly tell the difference between them and the mud flats they are attempting to master. ∎

Klootscheeten is a completely different affair. Literally translated, the word means "shooting lumps", whereby "shooting" makes the sport sound more dangerous than it is. The *Kloot* or "lump", a wooden ball measuring 2 inches in diameter and weighted down with lead, is not fired but thrown by hand. The favourite place for *Klootscheeten* competitions are the frozen fields and meadows in winter. The sport probably most similar to *Klootscheeten* is Alpine curling. The East Frisian variety uses much simpler devices; a curling stone is by far the more sophisticated of the two sporting implements.

Boßeln is more than just a casual pastime, played with great zest and enthusiasm as a team sport.

The aim of Boßeln is to reach the finish with the least number of throws of the wooden ball. Who'll win today?

Farm life in East Frisia. Pastural agriculture is largely predominant in the great expanses of marshland.

Trim thatched roofs, gables with crossed horses' heads and idyllic country scenes seem to dominate the landscape.
Yet agriculture in East Frisia is slowly dying.

Leer, the "gateway to East Frisia". Opposite the town hall is "Die Waage" (scales), where merchandise was sold by weight until 1946. The building with its hipped roof was once at the heart of town activity (main photo).

The Martin Luther House reminds us of the 16th century, when Protestant refugees fled to the area from The Netherlands, occupied by Spanish Hapsburgs (top). A period of prosperity saw the construction of magnificent town houses, such as Haus Samson (1643), which now accommodates a remarkable collection of porcelain, tiles and furniture (centre right and below).

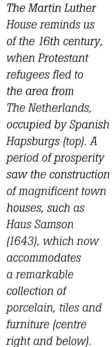

EAST FRISIANS MAKE HISTORY

East Frisia is not without its celebrities. Klaus Störtebeker, the Robin Hood of the German coastline, is an early example of local hero. The pirate was beheaded in 1401, but his popularity lived on. There are still many towns and villages today who claim to be his place of birth or to at least have sheltered him from henchmen.

More recent East Frisian history has also produced a few famous personalities. At least two men born in Emden are guaranteed a permanent place in Germany's memory. Henri Nannen, for example, a committed journalist and art collector, helped re-establish the German media after the Second World War. And Otto Waalkes, no less committed in the field of comedy and film and television entertainment, has proved that East Frisians are not only good for having jokes told about them – they also have a sense of humour. Henri Nannen launched *Stern* in 1949. What started out as a youth magazine was now very much geared towards an adult readership. The first issue displayed a scantily-clad Hildegard Knef on its cover,

a bold move for prudish post-war Germany but one which proved profitable. Under Nannen's management, first as editor-in-chief and then as publisher, *Stern* became the magazine with the highest circulation in Europe. But in later years, Nannen was deeply hit by the scandal of the forged Hitler diaries, published in *Stern,* and left the publishing house in 1983. Only one year before he had presented his home town of Emden with an art gallery which rapidly achieved fame well beyond provincial boundaries. Here you can still marvel at Nannen's magnificent collection of

art in Hamburg his sense of fun drove him to take to the stage in 1972. His success is marked by coveted prizes such as the Bambi, Ehrenlöwe, Goldene Kamera, Goldene Schallplatten and platinum awards. Hundreds of thousands of copies of his books are sold, his films draw millions to the cinema and Emden is so proud of its very own comedian that

Probably East Frisia's most prominent personality: Otto Waalkes. He first saw the light of day in 1948 in Emden.

in 1987 it opened the "Otto-Huus"

with Otto Waalkes' signature in its "Golden Book".

modern art which he personally oversaw until shortly before his death.

And Otto? Shortly after he was born, his mother is supposed to have said to Herr Waalkes: "Hasn't he got sweet little feet?" To which came the succinct reply: "Compared to his face, yes." This conversation undoubtedly never took place but causes much merriment in Otto's films and is typical of Otto's sense of humour. He loves to laugh at himself and his fellow countrymen and women. Otto has adopted the underlying theme of most East Frisian jokes, namely that the people in the region belong to a strange species; in one of his sketches he talks about an imaginary book entitled *Rearing and Caring for your East Frisian*. Otto Waalkes made his first public appearance as the guitarist of the Rustlers. After spending a few terms studying

Dat Otto Huus

Dat Otto Huus

in Emden

Große Straße 1 / Postfach 1345

Monument and store for a living legend: the Otto House in Emden.
Open Mon–Fri 9.30 a.m.–6 p.m., Sat 9.30 a.m.–1 p.m. late Sat until 4 p.m. Apr–Oct also Sun 10 a.m.–4 p.m. Tel. + 49 (0) 49 21/21 21.

Emden has a rich history as a harbour town and port of trade. The "Deutsche Bucht" lightship, now a restaurant, is anchored in the harbour. The town hall with its classic Renaissance façade was erected in 1576 and today houses the local East Frisian Museum (well worth a visit). Emden is East Frisiaís largest town and the centre of local industry.

The fish market is an interesting port of call for tourists and locals alike, vending delicacies for regional dishes and quick snacks.

A typical pose for "Old Fritz" (Frederick the Great), gazing west from Knock. East Frisia experienced a lasting cultivation of the area under the Prussians, who were pursuing their coastal interests.

Ditzum, with its 700 inhabitants, is the last fishing harbour on the East Frisian Ems and one of the pearls of the region.

Pretty Greetsiel in a sea bay is probably the most beautiful fishing village on the North Sea. Houses with pointed gables and red cobbled streets draw tourists as readily as the twin windmills in their idyllic setting a little out of town (main photo). There are also plenty of wonderful church organs to be found in East Frisia, such as here in Greetsiel; eleven of them were constructed by the famous Hamburg organ builder Arp Schnitger (1648-1719).

WHALERS, SEAL HUNTERS AND SHRIMPERS

ready for throwing

*in the flesh of
the escaping animal*

*from left to right:
seal clubs
3 blubber knives
2 spears*

Life on the coast is tough – and was even tougher in years gone by. The constant wind and relatively short summers often meant a poor harvest on land. The sea was thus the main source of nourishment until well into the twentieth century. Yet the ocean wasn't forthcoming with its bounty; it had to be hunted in fishing expeditions which often endangered the lives of the fishermen, armed with harpoons, clubs, knives and nets.

It is interesting to note that the East Frisians hardly ever set out to sea in their own boats. They signed on with the fishing fleets of their neighbours to the east and west. For centuries, whales and seals were the best catch. Products made from these animals sold extremely well. The fishermen sailed far out to sea in simple sailing boats. If they saw a whale, then rowing boats were quickly lowered into the water and the men tried to get within harpooning distance of their prey. At first the fight was evenly matched, with many men dying in the process. In the end it was usually the whale who lost the bloody battle. Whale blubber and sperm oil were valuable commodities. And if the hunters were especially lucky, they might find ambergris, a rare, fragrant cholesterol product, in a dead sperm whale. This promised extra profits, for the much sought-after, grey, waxy substance was used in those days for medicinal purposes, to relieve cramps and to stimulate the body, the appetite and the digestive system. At the end of the fishing trip, profits were split according to an ingenious system, whereby the ship owners and the captains were the main beneficiaries …

Seal hunting was very similar. Seals were hunted not so much for their meat but for their precious skins, especially those of young seals found basking in large colonies on sandbanks and the shore. One blow with the club, and the practised hunter could skin the dead or stunned seal with a few deft movements.

Better boats and more successful hunting methods were much to the advantage of human hunters. Fishing and preparation of the catch were soon fully industrialised. Yet decades of brutal hunting expeditions have taken their toll of the sea's apparently never-ending supply of aquatic produce. Now people are trying to preserve the variety of marine species and prevent this important source of food from completely drying up by imposing fish quotas, conservation orders and even international fishing bans. The descendants of the daring whalers and seal hunters of the past now concentrate on small fish and shrimps nearer to home. Despite strict quotas, the catch is becoming increasingly less profitable and many of the fishermen are giving up. Fishing in the small harbour towns in East Frisia is no longer of any economic significance. Only the tourists believe that the coast is not complete without its picturesque cutters surrounded by flocks of seagulls. ■

Prawns and shrimps are some of the most delicious fruits of the North Sea. Fishermen haul in their bounty from aboard a cutter.

Walfischlied

1. Wollt Ihr mal een Untier sehn,
   i o strampeli.
   Dann müßt Ihr hin nach Grönland gehn,
   strampeli o weh, o weh, o weh,
   strampeli o weh,
   du mein trulajeh strampeli o weh.
   strampeli o weh.

2. Komdür in't Kreinnest süht all'n Wal und brüllt nu „Fall! Fall! Öwerall!"

3. De Lüd de fallt nu in de Slup; den een blött de Näs, den annern de Snut!

4. De Walfisch is all wedder dor; Harpunen sust em um dat Ohr.

5. Se stekt em in dat fette Gnick, de Walfisch in de See sik dükt.

6. Op em! Se lanzt den Walfisch dot, de See de farwt sik blödig rot.

This whaling song from Glückstadt was sung by the locals when fishing in Greenland.

Cutter fishing is no longer the primary source of income it once was in Greetsiel and the other fishing villages lining the coast. Yet visitors continue to enjoy the romantic flair of the harbour and the many events, including the Drachenfest in September and the arts and crafts fair.

Many fishermen set out to sea from Norddeich.

A great place to visit is the seal sanctuary which rears motherless seal cubs ("bleaters") and also has an exhibition on mud flat habitats.

Norddeich is where ferries transport holidaymakers to Norderney and Juist, but with its own stretch of beach it also attracts visitors to what has become East Frisia's largest seaside resort.

East Frisia's most splendid Renaissance gable, built in 1576, can be found on Schöninghsches Haus in Norden (top right and left). The Ludgerikirche houses one of Arp Schnitger's best-sounding church organs.

Norden also boasts the Tea Museum and the Mennonite church in a refurbished patrician house from 1662 (bottom right).

TEA
AND "BEAN SOUP"

East Frisia wouldn't be East Frisia without tea, its national drink. Pro capita consumption here breaks all records.

The maps in the definitive gourmet guides to Germany show East Frisia as a blank area. Yet merely measuring quality with the taste of *haute cuisine* would be doing the region an injustice. East Frisia does offer its very own culinary bliss – to fish fans. The mud flats deliver delicious marine occupants almost right to your doorstep. Quality here is measured in freshness, something only the coast can guarantee.

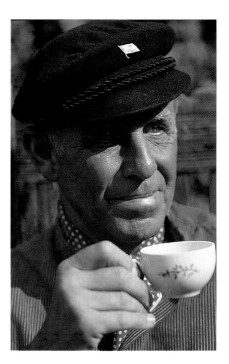

East Frisian "bean soup" *(Bohnensuppe)* is another kettle of fish altogether – albeit without fish. And the "beans" aren't beans but raisins, steeped in brandy and sugar; the longer the better. It used to be a local custom that fathers-to-be prepared a substantial portion of the brew well before the birth so that he and his male neighbours had something spirited to wet the baby's head with. Recipes handed down over the years omit one crucial instruction – how long to leave the concoction to mature. Perhaps they took the length of a pregnancy.

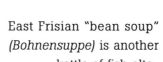

If you then deduct the few weeks where the father is unaware of his future role from the nine months, plus the time he needs to collate all the ingredients and mix up his potion, then there is still enough time for the *Bohnensuppe* to reach perfection.

Even a child born after seven months doesn't greatly reduce the drink's quality. One thing you should watch out for, however: East Frisian *Bohnensuppe* is not as harmless as it seems …

The most important beverage for the East Frisians (and it can be drunk any time!) is tea. They consume gallons of it. The statistics are impressive: over 5 pounds per person per year, or 1,600 cups, or 4.38 cups per day. And as babies and toddlers are normally not yet familiar with this liquid delicacy, the real per capita consumption is actually higher. The East Frisians also often use the tea leaves twice, refilling the pot; if you take these two factors into consideration, then the statistics lie far higher than official estimates.

importers and traders buy up the precious merchandise, store it and later sell it for the highest price they can get. The tea is then loaded onto lorries and taken to Germany's centre of tea consumption, East Frisia. Here the leaves are transformed into aromatic, unmistakable *Ostfriesenmischung* ("East Frisian blend"), primarily by the Ostfriesische Tee-Gesellschaft and the Teekanne company, who mix 80 – 90 % Assam with 10 – 20 % Ceylon or Darjeeling.

Sipping this lovingly-prepared, stylishly-served drink, it's not only the East Frisians who agree that the tea's long journey was well worth it! ∎

Stylish in its neat simplicity: brick façade in Greetsiel harbour.

Tea has a long journey before it can trickle down East Frisian throats. Packed in containers, it crosses the Indian Ocean, then the Red Sea, the Suez Canal, the Mediterranean and the North Atlantic and the North Sea before reaching the Elbe. It breaks its journey in Hamburg, where

East Frisian culture: teashop and museum in Greetsiel (left), living room in the Carolinensiel museum (centre) and the tearooms in the Moorland Museum (right).

Not far from the coast opposite Baltrum is Schloss Dornum, a local gem, built in 1698 as Norderburg Castle. The castle is "guarded" by a stone lion brandishing a coat-of-arms and to enter the main building you have to cross a wooden bridge. Concerts are often held in the main hall of the Baroque palace.

Fishing villages line the coast like a string of pearls. Even in winter they sparkle with their own particular charm: Hooksiel (top left) and Harlesiel (main photo).
It isn't only the shrimp cutters, such as this one in Neuharlingersiel (bottom left), which attract the visitors. The villages and their houses also cut a fine architectural figure.

*The harbour museum
in Carolinensiel
depicts how houses
and shops used to be
arranged inside,
such as this historic
chemist's (top right).*

*This navigational light
(above) guides ships into
Wilhelmshaven. Tankers
carrying crude oil are
frequent visitors here. The
harbour and town owe their
founding to the imperial
navy of the 19th century
(1856–1869).*

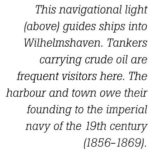

Not actually part of East Frisia, but not far away: Frisian Jever, part of the Oldenburg district, with its palace. The domed tower was erected atop an old castle keep from 1428 (top left). The modern brewery (top right) gleams in stark contrast.

WATER, WIND AND SAND

Ebb and flow are eternal forces. They are strengthened or weakened by the wind and the phases of the moon, but always effective. In the wake of their permanent exchange coastline and islands are formed. The sea washes up and down the shore twice a day. The average difference between high and low

Nature is constantly seeking its dues. Breakwaters try to protect the land from the sea's permanent attacks.

tide at Wilhelmshaven is about 13 feet. Yet storm tides can lash water levels up to more than 10 feet above the normal high tide levels and quickly become dangerous.

There is no island or stretch of coastline lacking in bitter experience.

Nature has redesigned the coastal map time and time again. Islands have been drastically reduced in size or even torn apart. Entire areas of land have disappeared. People, animals and houses have been swallowed by the waves. In the devastating flood tides of February 1962 alone, several hundred people lost their lives.

The sea takes away, but also gives. The East Frisian islands are a gift of the sea. The tides constantly transport large amounts of sand which are gradually deposited, forming sandbanks. These are at first only visible at low tide. Further tides deposit more sand, building up banks which remain dry at high tide. Sea birds drop plant seed on the banks, and the wind also blows seed over from the mainland. Robust plants such as marram grass grow on the barren soil. The roots of plants which survive strengthen the loose, sandy ground. Plants seed themselves in the lee of their stalks. The sandbanks grow and gradually dunes are established. More demanding plants start to

grow on the dune side sheltered from the wind, firming and enriching the soil. An island is born.

Shallows lie between the islands and the shore. Each high tide washes suspended matter and sand onto the sea bed and deposits it there.

At low tide the water recedes along narrow channels and straits and the mud flats are largely dry. Only then does the sea allow nature enthusiasts to explore its watery bed. The huge flocks of sea birds looking for food on the flats betray that the grey mud is full of life.

Yet only an expert is able to point out the great diversity

of this habitat to the visitor. The microfauna buried in the mud and along the tideline offers plenty of nourishment for crabs, worms, mussels, winkles and fish. They in turn offer a rich platter for the sea birds: waders and gulls, the latter everywhere, crying for food all along the coast and shallows. For safety reasons it is not advisable to go out on the flats alone. Being surprised by the tide coming in, sinking into deep mud or getting caught in one of the tidal channels can be fatal.

Nature lays down its laws more clearly on the coast than inland. Changes can be seen more quickly. There is constant coming and going, give and take – a permanent growing and fading away. ▪

The mud flats are exposed at low tide. Water remains only in narrow, sandy channels. Shallows markers guide boats and ships at high tide.

The mud flats are home to a rich variety of species. Yet you have to look closely to discover the shy inhabitants of this watery animal kingdom.

The East Frisian islands and their seaside towns are tourist magnet number 1. Norderney in the extreme west of the island of the same name (top left and centre) is chic – and has the oldest resort on the North Sea coast from 1797. Whereas most of the islands are narrow and elongated, Borkum is less typically round in shape (bottom left).

Elegant is perhaps the word to describe Borkum's north beach, with its three miles of promenade and gleaming white hotels from the turn of the century (main photo). The extremely long and thin Juist (top right) is just the opposite: the "tranquil isle", formerly known as the "magic land".

Singer Lale Andersen made a home for herself on Langeoog and was held in high esteem by the islanders. There is a wonderful view from Melkhorn dunes, at 68 feet above sea level East Frisia's highest point.

All of the islands offer wind, water and sandy beaches. Despite these similarities, each of the islands has its own character. Baltrum (left) is the smallest of the lot and is known as the "Sleeping Beauty of the North Sea".

Following double spread: although for administrative purposes Wangerooge is not actually an East Frisian island, it undoubtedly belongs to the chain. The new lighthouse has taken on the job of the old one, which can now be visited and climbed. The massive west tower has had a rather more varied career, serving as a prison for part of its history.

Wangerooge with the old lighthouse (top). The west of the island is heavily defended against the permanent suck of the sea (main photo). The "green isle" of Spiekeroog is pretty much as it always was and offers peace and tranquillity (centre left). Here public transport is provided by horse-drawn trams (bottom left).

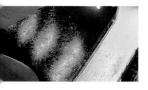

WHERE OCEAN LINERS GLIDE THROUGH FIELDS OF GREEN

The largest shipbuilding shed in Europe is at Meyer shipyards in Papenburg on the Ems River.

Meyer has primarily made an international name for itself with its huge ferries and cruise liners.

Building special ships requires a high level of expert knowledge. Naval architects advocate safe construction and quality.

The Emsland, the stretch of land along the Ems River, is less well-known and only partially belongs to East Frisia. Its real charm is hidden far away from the motorway along which most tourists speed northwards to their East Frisian holiday. The stretch of magnetic railway currently being tested here is

also dedicated to high velocities. Yet neither method of transport can divulge the beauty of this peaceful part of the country. For this you need a bicycle and plenty of time. Then you can enjoy even the most remote corners of the Emsland along the excellent network of cycling paths here. A few years ago the Emsland was almost devoid of tourists. Yet in recent times the Meyer shipyard in Papenburg has helped boost popularity. In an area known for its weak economy, the successful ship builders have started constructing cruise liners, one larger than the other, for tourists wanting

to travel the world's oceans. In contrast to the generally ailing shipbuilding industry, Meyer is able to boast order books bursting with commissions. The way from the Papenburg shipyard to the sea is along the Ems – a small river not really large enough to cope with Meyer's seafaring mammoths.

Some time ago Meyer's shipyard – with the largest shipbuilding shed in Europe – was asked by an English ship owner to build the *Oriana*.

The naval architecture presented little difficulty

for the industrious Papenburgers, but they hit problems when it came to delivery. The Ems simply wasn't deep enough. As the luxury liner gradually grew, fishermen, environmentalists and political parties of all colour and status right up to provincial government level heatedly

The building of the Oriana caused quite a stir throughout the land. The Ems had to be deepened for it to be able to travel from Papenburg to the coast.

debated the practicalities and non-sense, the good and evil of deepening the river. At the end of the day, economy won over ecology (as it usually does), especially as Meyer publicly toyed with the idea of moving its business away from the Emsland.

After much arguing, the Ems was finally deepened just in time to allow the *Oriana* to spectacularly glide through the Ems meadows towards the North Sea. Had the debate been settled in favour of the environment, then the ocean giant would still be stuck at Meyer's shipyard as a painful reminder of the shipping industry's lost battle. Hardly had the ship been delivered and christened amidst much ceremony by the Queen when Meyer received an even bigger order. The Ems faced disruption once again. A repeated digging project would, however, hardly be politically viable. The solution was a proposed river barrage to the tune of 50 million Deutschmarks. This would dam the river and create an area of water deep enough at the shipyard. Those in favour of the barrage argue that it would offer protection in the event of flooding. A clever move which appears to demonstrate consideration for local inhabitants, thus placating would-be opponents … ∎

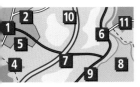

EAST FRISIA AT A GLANCE

1 Buddelschiff-Museum

How did the ship get in the bottle? More than 150 **artistic ships in bottles** are on display here, most of them scaled, faithful models of all kinds of ships from skiffs to windjammers in various glass containers, some holding up to 13 gallons. Many of the exhibits were fashioned aboard sailing boats in the 19th century. The museum also has an extensive collection of impressive ship pictures.

(Neuharlingersiel, Am Hafen Westseite 7. Open daily except Tues. April–Oct. 10 a.m.–1 p.m. & 2 p.m.–5.30 p.m.)

Bottled works of art: the ship in the bottle is a fascinating artefact.

2 "Deutsche Bucht" Lightship

The former lightship was anchored and manned for 65 years (until 1983) in the Deutsche Bucht near Helgoland. Work aboard the 172-foot-long boat was especially hard in the long winter months. This monument to **maritime technology** has weighed anchor for the last time in Emden; it is well worth visiting and now houses a **restaurant** with an interesting atmosphere.

(Emden, Rats-Delft, tel. +49-(0) 49 21-2 23 73)

Lightships were floating light-houses. There haven't been any manned navigational aids for years now.

3 Manningaburg Open-Air Museum

Manningaburg, a moated castle from the 15th/16th century, was made a museum in the mid-1980s. The castle was once owned by the Frisian Manninga dynasty and the Cirksena counts. The museum gives **details of the history of the two families** and in an exhibition entitled "From Tower House to Fortress" traces the **history of chieftains' residences and castles in East Frisia.**

(Pewsum, Drostenplatz. Open 15 May–15 Oct. Tue & Thur 10 a.m.–12.30 p.m. and 3 p.m.–5 p.m., Sat & Sun 3.30 p.m.–5 p.m.)

4 Greetsiel

This former little **fishing village** on the Ems estuary has spruced itself up for its guests. With its twin-windmill land-mark, this pretty town attracts more visitors than any of the other fishing ports nearby. Greetsiel is nevertheless not to be missed and is well-prepared for the flood of tourists. There's always room in one of the pubs or restaurants here to enjoy the finest shrimps or fish fresh from the sea.

5 "Alter Leuchtturm" Island Museum

Wangerooge's old lighthouse (built in the mid-19th century) was in service until 1969. The gallery of the building, almost 130 feet high, looks out over the East Frisian islands to the west, over flat, green plateaux to the south and across the North Sea as far as Helgoland – **the views are impressive.** The ground floor houses a small **museum on the history of the island** with artefacts from the fishing industry and bird world. *(Zedeliusstraße. Local notices give opening times, or ring +49 - (0) 44 69 -89 40 and -89 64)*

6 Kunsthalle

Henri Nannen not only made a name for himself as a journalist and the editor of *Stern* magazine, but also as a collector and patron of art. He bequeathed his significant collection of paintings, graphics and sculptures to his home town of Emden and donated a suitable building to house them. Nannen's collection includes a great number of **works by German Expressionists,** and the museum also stages **various exhibitions on 20th-century art.** Children can join in holiday art courses at the museum's art school. *(Hinter dem Rahmen 12-14. Open: Tue 10 a.m.–8 p.m., Wed-Fri 10 a.m.– 5 p.m., Sat & Sun 11 a.m.–5 p.m. Art school tel. +49 - (0) 49 21-3 28 80, fax -2 86 67)*

7 Moor- und Fehnmuseum Elisabethfehn

The **Moorland and Fen Museum** and its grounds offer a comprehensive insight into themes typical of the region, namely **moorland, the peat trade and the fens**. The spectrum ranges from flora and fauna on the fens, from how moorland is formed, used and protected to how difficult it was for people to live and work here. Exhibits include tools, typical moorland housing and bog bodies *(26676 Barßel, Oldenburger Straße 1. Open Tue–Sun 10 a.m.–6 p.m.).*

8 Ostfriesisches Landesmuseum

The East Frisian Museum in the wonderfully restored town hall in Emden harbour has a very interesting **display on prehistoric times and early history and the history of Emden and its surrounding area**. No other museum offers such a comprehensive presentation of East Frisian history. The museum is annexed to the Emden **Rüstkammer (armoury)** which supplied men-at-arms until the end of the 18th century. The collection of weapons and armour is first class.
(Emden, Neutorstraße. Open April–Sept. Mon–Fri 10 a.m.–1p.m. & 2 p.m.–5 p.m.; April/May Sat & Sun 11 a.m.–1 p.m., June–Sept. Sat & Sun 11 a.m.–1 p.m.; Oct–Mar Tue–Fri 10 a.m.–1 p.m. & 3 p.m.–5 p.m., Sat & Sun 11 a.m.–1 p.m. Closed public holidays.)

9 Ostfriesisches Teemuseum

Tea is of great importance in East Frisia. Yet the **East Frisian Tea Museum** goes far beyond tea's regional history. The Oswald von Diepholz Collection spans the subject of tea from its **origins in China** to how it came to Europe and **modern tea-drinking ceremonies**. Nothing is left out, from advertising, sales and tea processing to aromatic *Ostfriesenmischung*. The collection also exhibits **tea utensils** from various countries and periods.
(Norden, Am Markt 36. Open Mar–Oct., Tue–Sun 10 a.m.–4 p.m.)

10 The Störtebeker Trail

For those wanting to really explore East Frisia, try tracing Störtebeker's footsteps. There is hardly a village or town along the coast that doesn't lay claim to having sheltered the infamous pirate from Hanseatic henchmen. The **Störtebeker Tower in Marienhafe** is one of the supposed hiding places still visible today. Originally six floors high, the tower is the sad remainder of what was once a splendid church.

Störtebeker, the infamous pirate, is supposed to have sought sanctuary from his Hanseatic pursuers in this tower in Marienhafe.

1 10

The numbers 1–10 refer to positions marked on the map on the inside front and back covers.

CHRONOLOGICAL TABLE

12 BC

The word Frisian appears for the first time as *Frisones* in a Roman chronicle. It is used to describe a West Germanic tribe whose original area of settlement is not quite clear.

7th century AD

Frisians under King Radbod settle in the broad strip of land along the North Sea coast between Bruges in the west and the Weser River in the east, forming Frisia's largest territory.

8th century AD

The Franks put an end to the Frisian empire. Charlemagne orders that the north be converted to Christianity and the empire rapidly crumbles.

There are lots of castles and tribal residencies scattered all over East Frisia, such as Lütetsburg Castle.

C. 1000

Building of a "golden ring of dykes" to protect the countryside is started.

From 1200 onwards

Frisia is split into West, Middle and East Frisia. East Frisia covers the area between the Lauwers and Weser rivers. Political unity is lacking; the area is divided up into numerous *terrae,* or small rural republics, governed by elected consuls.
In order to prevent their independence from being lost under the rule of covetous princes, the East Frisians unite at Aurich and form the *Upstalsboomverband.*
The Upstalsboom pyramid is today a reminder of this alliance and a symbol marking the Frisians' successful defence of their freedom.

The Upstalsboom near Aurich is something of a regional relic and symbol of Frisian freedom.

14th century

Rulers calling themselves chieftains seize power locally; the area undergoes long periods of unrest and feuding.

1446 Powerful chieftain Ulrich Cirksena manages to unite the various small Frisian republics, first as an imperial county and later as the Principality of East Frisia. The areas to the west of the Ems fall to Burgundy. Ulrich's son, Edward I, is able to maintain the alliance and expand East Frisian territory.

The outer bailey and gate tower of Lütetsburg Castle near Hage were constructed in the Renaissance.

2nd half of the 16th century

Battles between the Lutheran ruler and the estates ruled by Emden weaken East Frisia in the third generation of the Cirksena dynasty.

1600 The Cirksenas acquire the Harlingerland.

1618–1648

East Frisia is devastated in the Thirty Years' War.

1633 Emden traders start cutting peat in Großefehn, making the first commercial use of the fens.

1654 The emperor supports East Frisian unity by making Count Enno Ludwig Cirksena a prince. The last Cirksena to rule East Frisia is Charles Edward.

1744 Following the death of the last of the Cirksenas, Frederick the Great marches into East Frisia. Hohenzollern troops had already taken control of Greetsiel in 1693. East Frisia becomes a Prussian province.

1800 A seaside resort is opened in Norderney.

1806–1813

After the Prussians are defeated by Napoleon, East Frisia is first given to The Netherlands and four years later to France.

1815 Prussia hands East Frisia over to Hanover at the Vienna Congress against the will of the East Frisians.

1866 East Frisia again comes under Prussian rule.

1942 East Frisia is given a new constitution according to the "Führer principle" by the National Socialists.

1944 Emden's old town is completely destroyed in an air raid.

1946 Under the official title of "Regierungsbezirk Aurich" (Aurich district), East Frisia becomes part of the new federal state of Lower Saxony.

Simple but beautiful: gable in Greetsiel.

Haneburg Castle in Leer is a splendid product of the wealth and glory of past rulers.

Following double spread: Papenburg is situated on the edge of East Frisia on the Ems River. Pretty bascule bridges straddle the waterways of the longest and oldest fen colony in Germany, founded to farm the surrounding moors.

OSTFRIESLAND

O s t f r i e s i s c h e

Baltrum

Norderney

Norderney

Juist

Dornume

Borkum

Neßmersiel

Borkum

Norddeich

Westermarsch

Norden

9

70

Marienhafe

Greetsiel **4**

Pilsum

10

Groothusen **3**

Moordorf

Upleward

Pewsum **8**

Ihlow

Rysum

6

46

2 **Emden**

Ditzum

Jemgum

NL

Bunde

Weener

70

31

Papen

1	Buddelschiff-Museum
2	Feuerschiff „Deutsche Bucht" (v.a. gutes Fisch-Restaurant)
3	Freilichtmuseum Manningaburg
4	Schönster Sielhafen
5	Inselmuseum „Alter Leuchtturm"
6	Kunsthalle
7	Moor- und Fehnmuseum Elisabethfehn
8	Ostfriesisches Landesmuseum
9	Ostfriesisches Teemuseum
10	Marienhafe, Störtebekerturm

Stürtz–REGIO.
Practical, packed with
illustrations – great souvenirs.
Stürtz Verlag GmbH,
Beethovenstraße 5,
97080 Würzburg, Germany

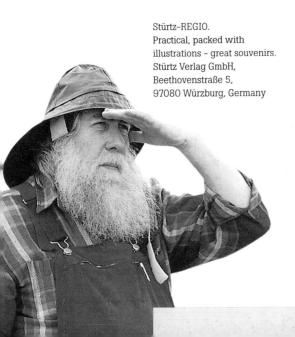